Women in Science Coloring and Activity Book

For Women in Biology, Women in Chemistry, and Women in Physics

Illustrated by Danielle Pioli

Science Wide Open series written by Mary Wissinger

Science, Naturally!
An imprint of Platypus Media, LLC
Washington, D.C.

Women in Science Coloring and Activity Book:
For Women in Biology, Women in Chemistry, and Women in Physics
Paperback first edition • September 2022 • ISBN: 978-1-938492-86-0

Illustrated by Danielle Pioli
Science Wide Open series written by Mary Wissinger
Original series concept by John J. Coveyou

Illustrations © 2022 Genius Games LLC

Cover Design: Caitlin Burnham, Washington, D.C.
Book Design: Marlee Brooks, Chevy Chase, MD
Editors:
    Marlee Brooks, Chevy Chase, MD
    Caitlin Burnham, Washington, D.C.
    Hannah Thelen, Silver Spring, MD

Enjoy all the titles in the Science Wide Open series
    Women in Biology • Las mujeres en la biología
    Women in Chemistry • Las mujeres en la química
    Women in Physics • Las mujeres en la física
    Women in Engineering • Las mujeres en la ingeniería
    Women in Medicine • Las mujeres en la medicina
    Women in Botany • Las mujeres en la botánica
    Women in Science Coloring and Activity Book
    More Women in Science Coloring and Activity Book

Published by:
    Science, Naturally! – An imprint of Platypus Media, LLC
    750 First Street NE, Suite 700
    Washington, DC 20002
    202-465-4798 • Pax: 202-558-2132
    Info@ScienceNaturally.com • ScienceNaturally.com

Distributed to the book trade by:
    National Book Network (North America)
        301-459-3366 • Toll-free: 800-462-6420
        CustomerCare@NBNbooks.com • NBNbooks.com
    NBN International (worldwide)
        NBNi.Cservs@IngramContent.com • Distribution.NBNi.co.uk

10 9 8 7 6 5 4 3 2 1

Printed in the United States.

Maria Sibylla Merian

Can you use your observation skills to find
the ten differences between these pictures?

Take a look outside. What living things do you see? Write or draw them below!

Hildegard of Bingen

Dawn Shaughnessy

Lab Goggles

Beaker

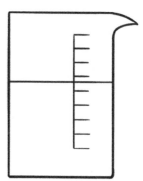

Pipette

Test Tube

Lab Coat

Can you match the scientists to their amazing discoveries? The first one is done for you.

Scientist:

Ada Yonath

Barbara McClintock

Linda Buck

Dawn Shaughnessy

Rosalind Franklin

Marie Curie

Chien-Shiung Wu

Discovered:

Smell receptors in the nose

The shape of DNA (a double helix)

The structure and function of ribosomes

6 new elements, including livermorium

The way atoms fall apart

Transposons or "Jumping Genes"

The radioactive elements radium and polonium

Laura Bassi

Jane Cooke Wright

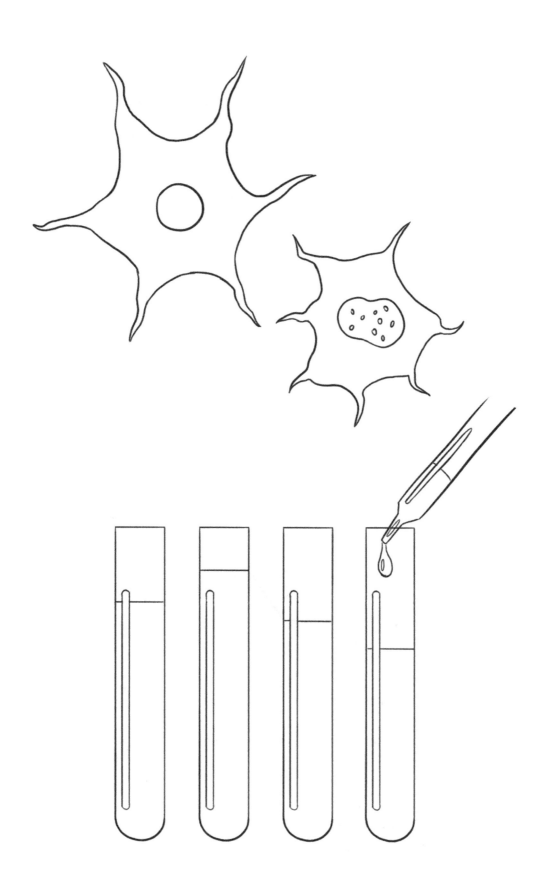

**Write down a hypothesis,
then test it out!**

Hint: A hypothesis is a guess about something that you think is true, which needs to be tested to find out if you are right. Your hypothesis could be that a gummy bear falls faster than a potato chip. You could test this with a friend by using a stopwatch to time how long it takes each item to hit the floor when you drop them from the same height.

Cleopatra the Alchemist

Marie Curie

The Periodic Table of Elements

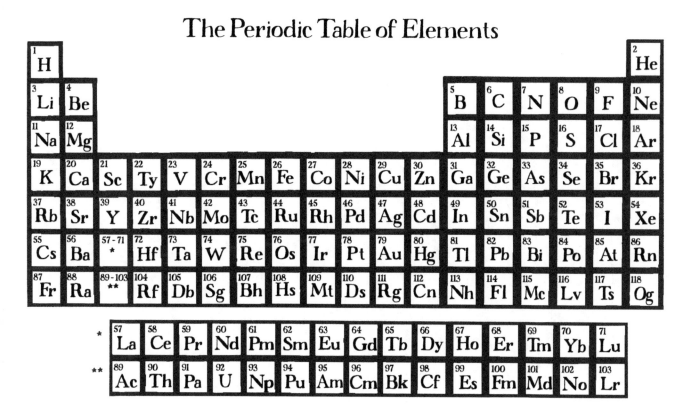

Can you circle:

Helium (He)?	Calcium (Ca)?
Silver (Ar)?	Nitrogen (N)?
Radium (Ra)?	Potassium (K)?
Oxygen (O)?	Hydrogen (H)?

Rosalind Franklin

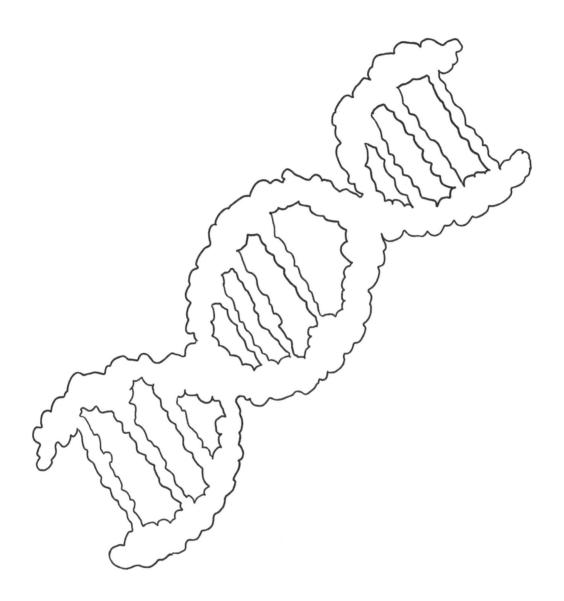

What is the structure of DNA?

Cone   Double Helix

Cylinder   Sphere

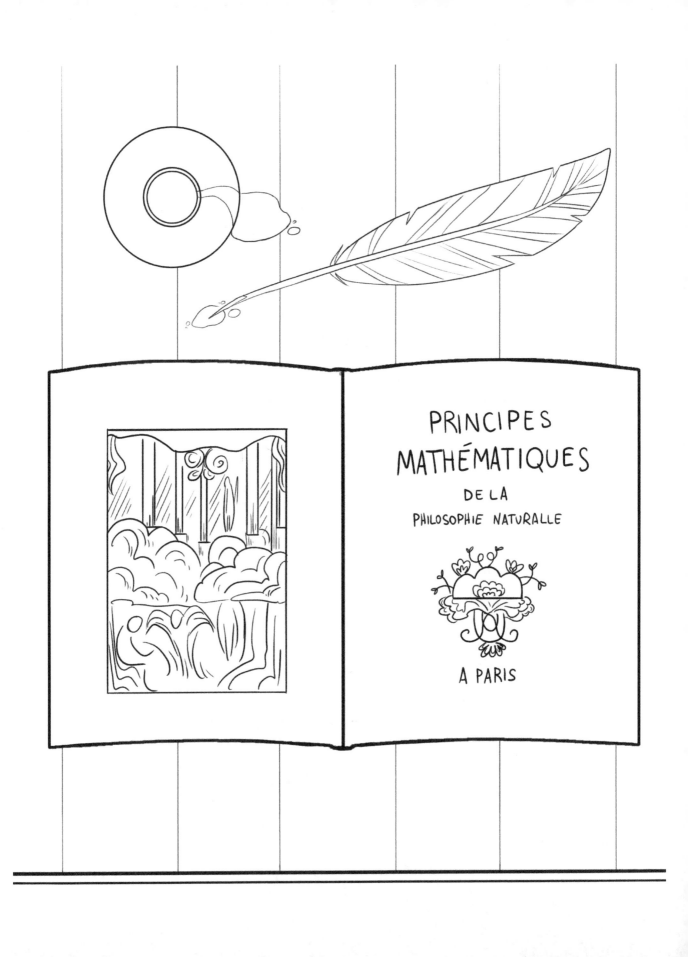

Émilie du Châtelet

Linda Buck

Draw something you've observed!

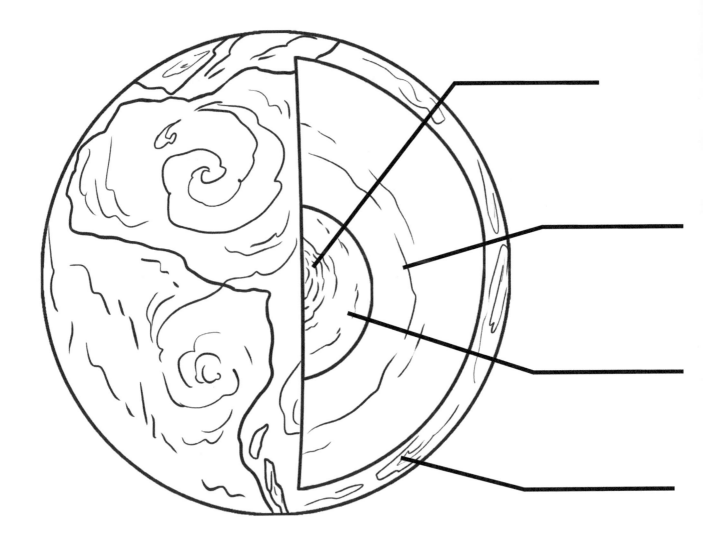

Can you label the layers of the Earth?

Mantle	Inner core
Outer core	Crust

Marie-Anne Paulze Lavoisier

Marie and Irene Curie

Barbara McClintock

Ada Yonath

Chien-Shiung Wu

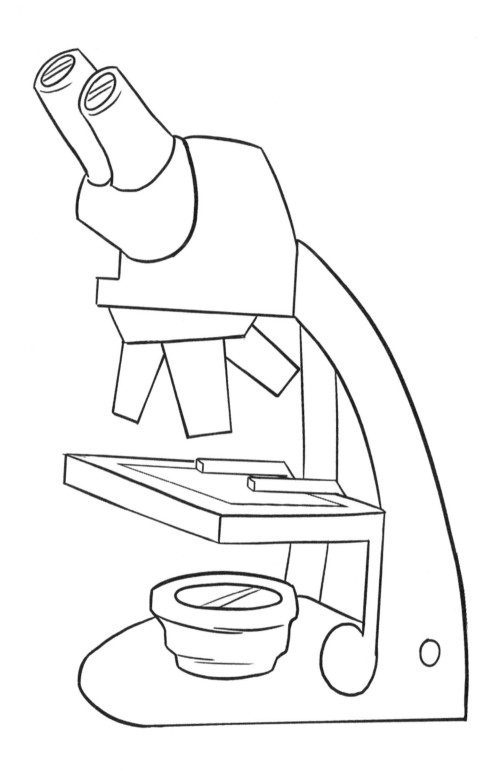

What are some examples of gravity you've observed?

1. _____

2. _____

3. _____

4. _____

5. _____

Nucleus

Rough ER

Smooth ER

Mitochondria

Golgi
Apparatus

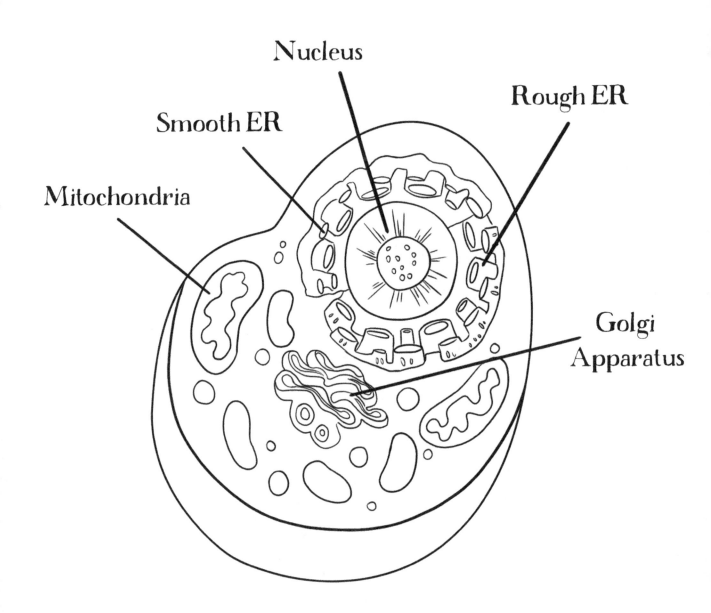

Can you draw the inside of a cell?

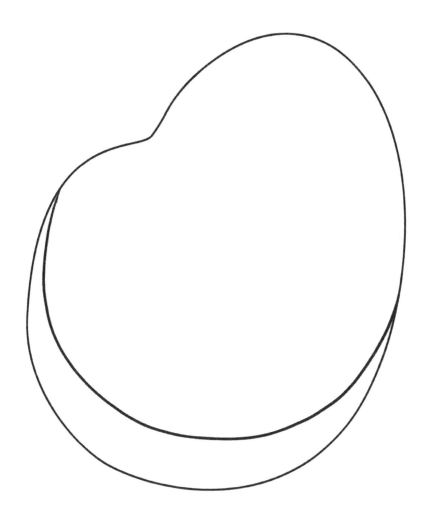

Color the electrons ⊖ yellow.
Color the protons ⊕ red.
Color the neutrons ◯ blue.

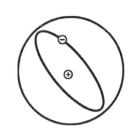

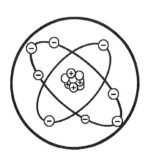

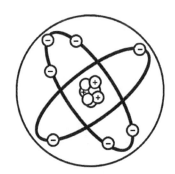

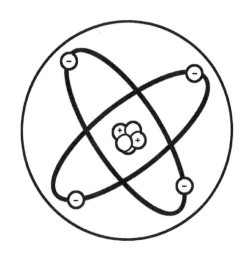

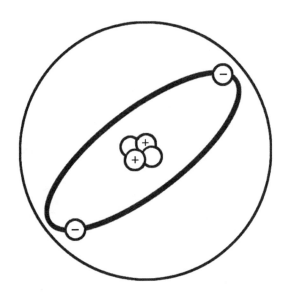

Hint: Electrons travel around the outside
of the atom. Protons and neutrons are both
found in the center of the atom, usually in
equal numbers.

Who made these prints? Draw the culprit!

Scientists are always asking questions
about how the world works!

What do you wonder about?

Discover the entire Science Wide Open series!

Hardback: $14.99 • Paperback: $12.95 • eBook: $11.99
8 x 8" • 40 pages • Ages 7-10

Book 1
Women in Biology

Hardback: 978-1-945779-09-1
Paperback: 978-1-938492-30-3
Spanish: 978-1-938492-07-5

Book 2
Women in Chemistry

Hardback: 978-1-945779-10-7
Paperback: 978-1-938492-31-0
Spanish: 978-1-938492-32-7

Book 3
Women in Physics

Hardback: 978-1-945779-11-4
Paperback: 978-1-938492-34-1
Spanish: 978-1-938492-35-8

Book 4
Women in Engineering

Hardback: 978-1-938492-52-5
Paperback: 978-1-938492-53-2
Spanish: 978-1-938492-95-2

Book 5
Women in Medicine

Hardback: 978-1-938492-55-6
Paperback: 978-1-938492-56-3
Spanish: 978-1-938492-96-9

Book 6
Women in Botany

Hardback: 978-1-938492-58-7
Paperback: 978-1-938492-59-4
Spanish: 978-1-938492-97-6

Women in Science
Coloring and Activity Book

A companion to books 1–3
ISBN: 978-1-938492-86-0

More Women in Science
Coloring and Activity Book

A companion to books 4–6
ISBN: 978-1-938492-87-7

Science, Naturally!
ScienceNaturally.com
Info@ScienceNaturally.com

 Sparking curiosity through reading